CW01302336

burntisland

ian farnes

ignitionpress

*for Layla & André*

First published in 2025
by **ignition**press
Oxford Brookes Poetry Centre
Oxford Brookes University
OX3 0BP

© Ian Farnes 2025

*Ian Farnes has asserted his right to be identified as author of this work
in accordance with the Copyright, Designs & Patents Act 1988.*

*This book is sold subject to the condition that it shall not, by way of trade or otherwise,
be lent, resold, hired out or otherwise circulated without the publisher's prior consent
in any form of binding or cover other than that in which it is published and without a
similar condition including this condition being imposed on the subsequent purchaser.*

Cover design: Flora Hands, Carline Creative

A CIP record for this book is available
from the British Library

ISBN 978-1-7394543-4-0

# Contents

| | |
|---|---|
| Key | 1 |
| After the Shift | 2 |
| Where the Moon Starts to Pull Like Some Far-off Engine | 3 |
| Resistant Cultures | 4 |
| Boundary Lines | 5 |
| Extractions | 6 |
| Tailings | 8 |
| Outside or Beyond | 10 |
| Catherine Unsung, 1916 | 11 |
| Free Spool | 12 |
| Apprenticeships | 13 |
| The Sun Shipping Co. Ltd. | 14 |
| Edna Adrift, 1992 | 15 |
| The Tar Brae | 16 |
| Peggy Forever, 1952 | 17 |
| The Berries | 18 |
| Sundials | 19 |
| High Tide | 20 |
| Winter | 21 |
| A Forest | 22 |

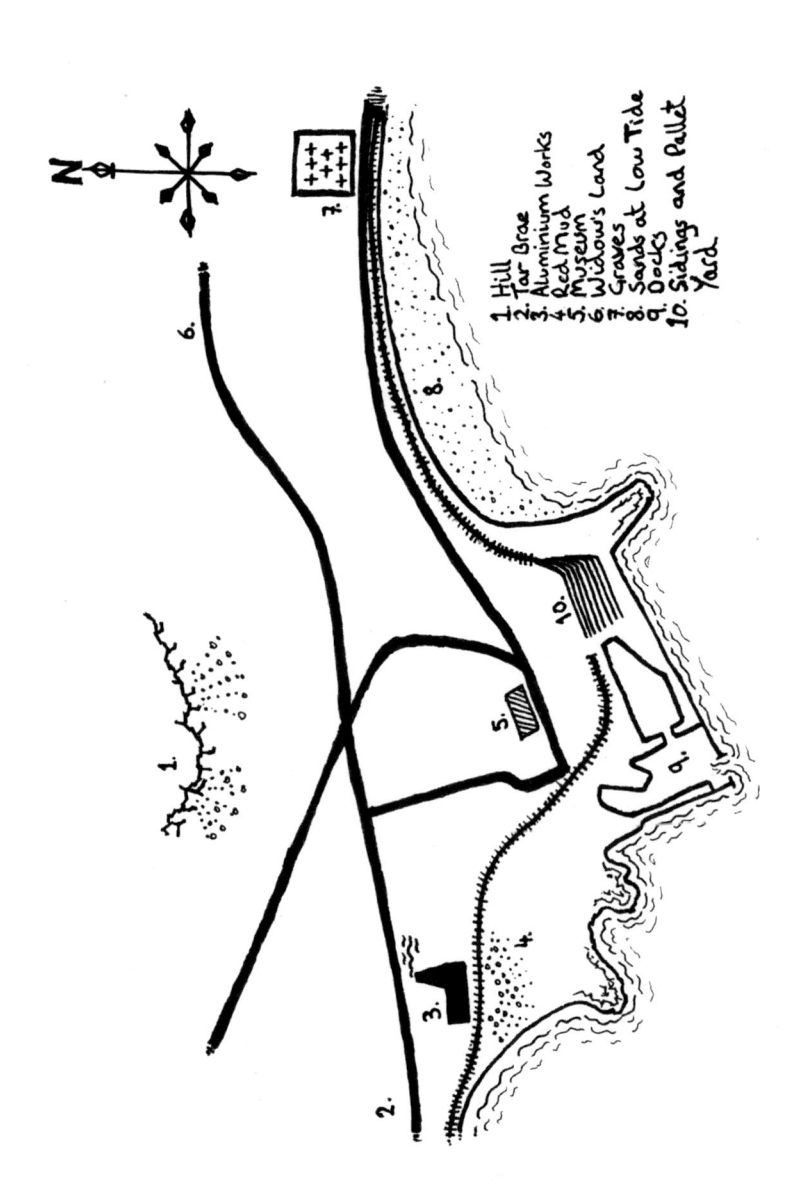

1. Hill
2. Tar Brae
3. Aluminium Works
4. Red Mud
5. Museum
6. Widow's Land
7. Graves
8. Sands at Low Tide
9. Docks
10. Sidings and Pallet Yard

*It was all coming back to him, as if the factory was his again... He went up to the hole in the kiln where he used to stand staring into the glowing mass. All he could see now was cold darkness.*

Sven Lindqvist, *Dig Where You Stand: How to Research a Job* (translated by Ann Henning Jocelyn)

## Key

I'm part of an exhibit in the local museum
a cardboard cut-out boy version of me
with hands on hips
in a plyboard Edwardian fair.

                  The path winds
                anticlockwise
          around a taxidermy lion
    a unicorn from a carousel
a map with streets I don't recognise
   plans for an abandoned village
        photographs of ships:
                Ohrmazd waiting in the docks
                    Leviathan at the ferry slip.

        If you want to see me
        talk to the librarian.
        She'll show you where the switch is
        and how to start the music.

# After the Shift

Half asleep
the hours drift and spread
meandering in cavities
leaking through weep holes

the beating
in the walls is the butcher
at his bones, re-limiting
the body. There's an ending
out by the harbour
where halyards clatter

and wind moves
through the warehouse
over yards of ivy, shards of glass
with gulls like tinfoil flecks
above the dawn bright
gable steps

          whirling into light
the swirl of mackerel tails
on concrete floors, fisheyes
shine like a full six million
glowing rivets on the bridge
or burning coals in engines
trailing vapour, all seen clear
as Granny Thompson's visions
of the dead upon the stage.

# Where the Moon Starts to Pull Like Some Far-off Engine

the shadow's body lengthens limbs in amber light
the weight of air narrows dusk down by the bridges

the other side of the pallet yard, the railway line

                dry sand, skims the surface
where the tide is drawn, carrying waders' calls
– not songs –
        to rag worms in the lug worm's mound

delicate

        a mud-crowned underworld, collapsing

molluscs in their shells

                dig
                        dig
                              the under

      pearl and under.

## Resistant Cultures

A dry wind carries the underwing's secret
sharp endings
filling lungs with breath of spores

in the first seeds, in splitting spurs
unlucky rivers
heave into the gutter on the way back home.

It might be a kindness to take us
from doghouse furnace
to the sidings: not yet brittle

but diamonds in the glitter dew
or mycelium threads
made hard in cold and wintering below

the shale tip ground, rich with veins
vermillion
working through the midden heap.

# Boundary Lines

In the clearing at the town's edge
is a stillness, woven into muted snowfall.
Two crows bolt black from the blank
flat skies and shift a hawk out, over
slate roofs, uphill to the miner's village
where we left the lines of rabbits' skulls
beside the broken wall.

# Extractions

It was Philip who tamed Richard's voice,
constructed it, building on its melody,
shortening its vowels, its Celtic overtones.

He took him to the mountain top
and tuned a voice, once dreadful,
hard to comprehend. He mastered it
with each word swung deep from pit of belly.
Richard almost sang

> *The Great Atlantic fault*
> *Starts in northern Spain*
> *It goes under*
> *The Bay of Biscay*
> *Comes up in South Wales*
> *And then again in Pennsylvania*

A richness in the seam

> *You could blindfold the miners*
> *They would still know the coalface*
> *My father would talk about it*
> *The way some men talk about women*
> *The beauty of the coalface*

A chasm opens

> *My father would look at the seam*
> *He would look at the seam of coal*
> *A black shining ribbon of coal*
> *And make a mark on it*

Richard puts a finger to his tongue
mimes making the mark.
He pretends to be his father.

*He'd say give me a number two mandrill*
*A half-headed pick*
*And if he hit it right*
*With one enormous blow*
*Twenty tonnes of coal*
*Would fall out of the coalface.*


My son's hand fits in mine
the soft give of the coastal path
his inheritance

sand soot-like black
washed in on waves
each percussive step
is a refrain.

## Tailings

I walk in snow-filled ruins taking photos,
brambles grown through window frames
a family home, then shiver on the threshold
      there's a sound, like drinking glasses
      brought together by a crowd

maybe it's an echo     something breaking
in the woods     the paths running through
get overgrown   misremembered

watching shadows dance
in fading streams of sunlight
I get caught between the footprints
of houses, school and music hall

the disused mines are hidden
and I can't make out
where shale was blasted from the seam
     or the downward slope
where British Alcan dumped red mud

after rain I'd try
to mould the clay-like lumps
      and feel them break
      between my fingers

      a childhood friend
    who died too young
is down at the stream
the red pond
scraping off-white foam from the bank
and letting the wind take it

maybe nothing's lost
in opening my hand to the clouds
holding the snow
and watching it fade like the trail
under the rising field.

## Outside or Beyond

Mother and child are waking on Widow's Land
lichen rosettes, glaucous white on the path
hold two lives intertwined.
The pale sun cracks the ice
in the drovers' track,
a fog hangs by the grey zinc lines
of barbed wire fences,
dewdrops hold on strands of wool
on stubble where the barley grew

> the baby's breath cracks
> at the back of the in-breath
> jawing at the morning
> calls in Crow Wood,
> calling back to days
> when we cut school
> and carved our register of absence
> in the sandstone.
>
> Place your fingers
> palm away, upon the neck
> of our young son
> back against the wind
> you find him sleeping
> in your arms and still

the elders at the standing stanes
hear the strain and whistle in the trees
> have faith
> the light can hold us.

# Catherine Unsung, 1916

*We have an anchor that keeps the soul*
*steadfast and sure while the billows roll*
*fastened to the rock which cannot move*
*grounded firm and deep in the saviour's arms.*

There are songs for those in peril
brooding on chaos deep and low
and rising with the tide.

On my mother's side a woman died
while giving birth
and all of us are carried by her blood.

She grew up near the Forth Bridge
saw it built
a black-boned skeleton of ox or stag.

When pregnant with her seventh child
she'd gone into the water, saved a boy
and in her portrait with its lead-backed frame
her painted pupils, black as breathless air
reach out
                like the river in low light
everything drawn to the deep
the space between the woven seagrass,
kelp bed,
sand eels, shoaling cod. We stagger

and are thrown onto the shore
like knotted wrack with holdfast broken
measuring the depths.

## Free Spool

If barely sounded lines run fast and straight
I'll keep the silence just as I've been taught,
get caught up in the stillness with my thoughts
they're yet to find their form
and won't be spat out like cheap hooks.
I'll find an ending
like when fish might swallow pellets
polished in the flesh of fists
then scattered on the seabed
sunk in silver bellies.
Lines cast out beyond the wall.
My scales will crystallise in salt
before I'm pulled to places
no-one wants to see.
I'll resist the dark
and find the silvered sea
like mussels in the deep

w
  h
    o
hide
their
truth
but
. not
as
w
  e
    l
  l
a
s
.  m
e

# Apprenticeships

Each of us an ark
a child
handed to the work

our arching prints
or whirling
looping fingertips

on golden films of oil
make rows
of metal filings

forming slow
magnetic fields
that fall to earth and flicker
in machine-shop lights.

A sleight of hand:
we see the metal's worth
and not what's broken.

# The Sun Shipping Co. Ltd.

&
sun field
sun bank
sun cliff
in first light at the landing's edge
were wrecks new risen
dotted lines on fading maps redrawn
porthole curtains twitching
on a ship that sailed

&
sun born
sun child
sun worn
whistles in the ears
with spines gone
red lead under nails
lines drawn on the surface of their skin
as cells divide in cigarette smoke
rays of sun split
shadows in the graving dock

&
sun field
sun bank
sun cliff
keels are laid in silt
their ribs are salt-corroded
colonies of rust

## Edna Adrift, 1992

there is a gap
between bedside
and water
a harbour's mouth
between pulp of fingers
feeling for edges
and the ridges
cut on crystal ashtrays
curved handles of enamel cups
crests of silver foil unwrapped
and cylinders of cigarettes
given to her majesty
an aspirin and a pulsing crown
smoke dispersing
in a ring of space
between the subject and her objects

lean into the flood
in darkening streams
with twists of hair and seaweed
in the moonwake crossing

# The Tar Brae

I try to believe the brae runs on
doesn't end in the grey mist
swallowing the islands
*Innis Coeddi, Innis Choluim*
rolling in from the Isle of May.

I try to remember the world on either side
but feel it letting go.
The jaw's hinge loosening
beneath my feet
the way things make me feel
    the touch        of waves
                    the water letting go
                    it never happened
                    I was never here.

                    Maybe the haar
                    hidden shores
                    or ghosts and spirits know
                    how ties are slipped
and rope unrolls  how islands drift
into the sea.

**Peggy Forever, 1952**

This blood is our blood
brought to her face
in the sun-hot glass works
sweat-stuck hair, peroxide blonde
with wages spent on rouge
eyeliner and satin shoes
a bus fare to the ballroom.

Lines of chairs by the hardwood floor
drapes and backcloth
frame the band in crisp white jackets
shirts and ties
making music for the dance.

Peggy sees the ceiling curve
plaster cherubs holding hands
gold leaf peacocks, tails displayed,
offering an olive branch
a promise of eternity

far beyond the winter gardens
distant ships with anchor lights
Edinburgh spun out of darkness
Pleiades threaded above.

# The Berries

There's a need for human hands
that feel the give of fruit
and take it without bruising.
You said the flesh of fruit was like ours,
pressed firmly. You know when it'll give
too much. I don't like to think of it.
I want sweetness without withering.

I'd love to love all summer long, but know
what grows from fruit that's done with;
nothing certain as the season's end. Maybe
now's the time to get to know the flesh
and live in spite of what's sprung from it
what falls, or moves beyond what's here:
to start to think of what's my own.

# Sundials

The oldest of them saw the shadow
pointing east from the transmitter

circled by a sea of wheat, an undulating breath
of wind across the water, in the fields
                            and on the skin.

The youngest had a finger in the gutter
of the cup and rings      in colour photographs

a ghosting flare         a halo
on the child             an orb of broken sun

caught up in youth      remembering
a heartbeat like a great dub echo

where we thought that we belonged but looked away

in daydreams           in the distance
the image started juddering and breaking

rolling lines uneven      changing rhythms
spooling loose on screen or lens or eye
or part of flame.

## High Tide

The first house in the town
had a garden
before the rows of graves

>busied by mussel pickers
>piercing turf
>with blood-coloured bills.

>>I look through the windows
>>of the house by the marsh
>>where the old man lived

painted on the door
is a fishing bird
with letters spelling *Holy Island*.

>Now his home is overgrown
>with sedge and reeds
>the water pools before the steps

>at the foot of the hill
>I begin the climb
>to where my family lived
>near winter fields

with gulls and crows
turned airward
by the oystercatchers.

## Winter

I will lie about the pieces of the story that are missing.

    Where the earth shifted underfoot,

        the headstone dominates.

The loam, the gold beneath the bracken cage,

        is stripped.

In children's gloaming dreams the liquid
tongue lies flat under an arc of hollowed trunk
and even when the auger cuts the roots,

    or white of spine, or knuckle on the litter

there's evidence that what was here needs
washed out clean

    that what might live nearby is close to sleep.

The rooks squat in their winter nests are folded
up in prayer,

        but once

they shook the dying leaves from silver
branches.

## A Forest

I heard it from my father's father:
how the giant spread
from forests of dead steel
through the gates in echoed imitations
each limb in step, the shimmering edge
in breeze and light, the loss of self in play.

Still the roots connect unseen and fibrous
underneath a centre I had mis-imagined
these clones shot from the mass
split dry from the bone behind,
degeneration visible

but I know that something grew here,
I can feel it move the slabs
beneath my feet
and work into the houses
on the new estate.

# Music

# Notes and Acknowledgements

The epigraph is taken from Sven Lindqvist's *Dig Where You Stand: How to Research a Job*, translated by Ann Henning Jocelyn (Repeater Books, 2023).

'Key' and 'The Sun Shipbuilding Co. Ltd.' both reference ship names. *Ohrmazd*, *Sunbank*, *Sunfield* and *Suncliff* were all made in Burntisland Shipyard with the contributions of my great grandfather, John Thompson, my great uncle, Robert Thompson, and my uncle, Andy Calder.

'Extractions' takes lines from an interview between Dick Cavett and Richard Burton, first aired on 8/4/1980.

The women referenced in the poems are Peggy Calder, née Thompson (my maternal grandmother, 1926–1976); Catherine Thompson (my maternal grandmother, 1926–1976); Catherine Thompson, née Marshall (my maternal great grandmother, 1901–1988); Catherine Marshall, née Fawcett (my maternal great, great grandmother, 1884–1916); and Edna Farnes, née Hall (1925–1992).

Special thanks to Niall Munro for his patience, encouragement and openness, and to the **ignition**press team for all of their work.

Thanks to the editors of *Gutter Magazine*, Issues 22 and 30; *Spelt*, Issue 4, *From Glasgow to Saturn*, Issue 49; *Lighthouse*, Issue 25 and to the editors of the anthology *The Last Song: Words for Frightened Rabbit*, where earlier versions of the poems included in this pamphlet appeared.

Thank you to the artist Hugh Matthews for his work on the map.

Thanks to Andy Clare for his friendship and his music.

Thanks to the members of the Burntisland Heritage Trust for all of their work which has informed much of mine in this pamphlet.

Huge thanks to my family, especially to my mother, Margaret, for all of her support and understanding. Without her stories this work would not have been started.

More than anyone, thanks must go to Layla Benitez-James, poet, partner and great love, for seeing something in me that no one else did.

FSC® C007326
MIX
Paper | Supporting responsible forestry

Oxford Brookes is committed to the environment.
This document is printed using processes that are:

**100%** Net Carbon Negative | **100%** Renewable Energy | **100%** ISO14001 | **100%** eco-friendly simitri® toner | **100%** Recyclable Stock | Zer**0**% *waste to landfill*

Printed by **seacourt** – proud to be counted amongst the top environmental printers in the world